friendship

ONE THING IN LIFE
YOU CANNOT DO ALONE

D. A. MICHAELS

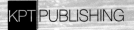

This is a book about friendship and the bonds that have been formed and proven over time. We have all had challenges throughout our lives, pressing forward knowing more will come—but we did not face those times alone. Someone was there to lift us up and remind us of our goals—to live another day and encourage others when their times of trouble come. It may have been someone you grew up with—your "best friend forever," a sibling, or a stanger who just "walked" into your life.

A sad, but true, fact is that the majority of men have, on average, less than one true friend. Regardless, man or woman, distance may have come between your friendship, and it's been some time since you have spoken to each other, or you have been wounded and you need to forgive, so you can heal and rekindle that connection.

Hopefully this book causes you to reflect and cherish the relationships that have formed in your life, rediscovering the joy and freedom "friendship" can bring—to laugh, to cry, and the freedom to enjoy life again with the ones you love and who love you. Someone *is* relying on you and you on them— you have been created to encourage and be encouraged. You are not alone. ❧ DM

FRIENDSHIP IS ALWAYS A SWEET RESPONSIBILITY, NEVER AN OPPORTUNITY.

KHALIL GIBRAN

The glory of friendship
is not the outstretched hand,
not the kindly smile,
nor the joy of companionship;
it is the spiritual inspiration
that comes to one
when you discover that someone else
believes in you and is willing
to trust you with a friendship.

RALPH WALDO EMERSON

A true friendship

is the best possession.

A Friendship Rekindled

I answered the phone and heard a voice say my name, a voice I didn't recognize. The person on the other end said, "Do you know who this is?" I admitted I didn't. I was elated when she told me.

She was an old friend and it had been over twenty-five years since I had heard her voice. I had helped her get her first job, encouraged her when she was learning to drive and was maid of honor at her wedding. After we both married, she and her husband had moved, to other towns, other states. We eventually lost touch.

Life gets busy. I had thought of her often. So much time had passed, maybe she didn't remember me and the good times we'd had. They were such a fun couple, and I was sure they had made many new friends.

As we talked, it was as if all those years had faded away and we were young girls again, laughing and talking about all the things we had done.

We keep in touch now and talk with each other regularly. We usually manage to see each other every year or so, even though we live hundreds of miles apart. I realize we have a special friendship that had continued to glow through all those years, and the flame is burning brightly again.

When we visit now over the phone, we have so many memories to share, it's as if those lost years had melted away. We know we have a relationship that will always endure. God had blessed us with a very special friendship. ※

A true friend is one

who knows all about you,

and still likes you.

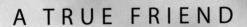

A TRUE FRIEND

will always greet you warmly.

BFF

**WITHOUT FRIENDS
NO ONE WOULD
CHOOSE TO LIVE,
THOUGH HE HAD
ALL OTHER GOODS.**

ARISTOTLE

Some friendships

break the genetic barrier.

Simple acts

can remind a person

that they are not alone ...

and that *you* call them

"friend."

I MAY NOT ALWAYS BE THERE WITH YOU, BUT I WILL ALWAYS BE THERE FOR YOU.

A friend loves at all times,

and a brother is born

for adversity.

PROVERBS 17:17 (NKJV)

Between true friends
words are optional.

Therefore, as the elect of God, holy and beloved,
put on tender mercies, kindness,
humility, meekness, longsuffering;
bearing with one another,
and forgiving one another,
if anyone has a complaint against another;
even as Christ forgave you, so you also must do.
But above all these things put on love,
which is the bond of perfection.

COLOSSIANS 3:12-14 (NKJV)

Blessed are they who have the gift

of making friends,

for it is one of God's best gifts.

It involves many things,

but, above all, the power

of going out of one's self

and appreciating whatever

is noble and loving in another.

THOMAS HUGHES

THE BETTER I GET TO KNOW MEN, THE MORE I FIND MYSELF LOVING DOGS.

CHARLES DE GAULLE

former president of the French Republic

Friendships can stand

the test of distance…

although I'd rather

you were *here* in person.

Together, we look like this.

**FRIENDSHIP IS LIKE
COFFEE BEANS.
MORE IS NOT BETTER
BUT BEST
WHEN HAND-SELECTED.**

Even the smallest gestures

from a friend

can encourage one enough

to make the worst day

spectacular!

We cannot tell the precise moment
when friendship is formed.
As in filling a vessel drop by drop,
there is at last a drop
which makes it run over;
so in a series of kindnesses
there is at last one
which makes the heart run over.

JAMES BOSWELL

Friendship is unnecessary,

like philosophy,

like art . . .

It has no survival value;

rather it is one of those things

which give value

to survival.

C. S. LEWIS

Best Friends

by SUE IKERD

Best friends are special,
     they're tough to explain
A true friend is a blessing
     that can be hard to attain

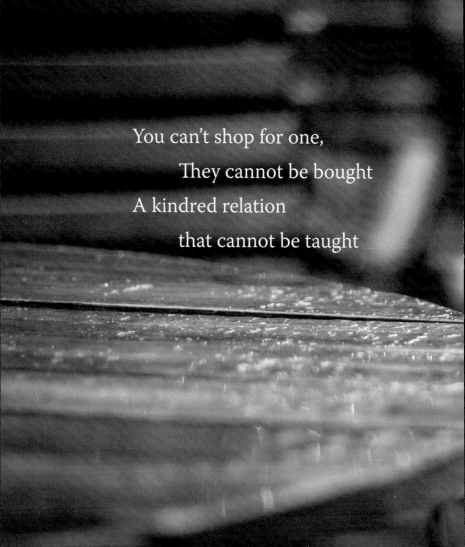

You can't shop for one,

 They cannot be bought

A kindred relation

 that cannot be taught

Someone to share secrets

and take long walks with

Call in the night

when you need someone to talk with

One who stands by you
in good times or bad
They know what to say
when you're happy or sad

It's like finding the gold
at rainbow's end
You have true wealth
when you find a best friend

※

Knowing *you*

are thinking

about *me*

makes being alone

easier.

BFF

Friendship is always better shared.

Friendship is *always* ready

to start

from where it left off.

It may be

an old-fashion method,

but talking to my best friend

is worth the wait—

and the whole roll of dimes!

True friendship
may start slowly . . .

but offers blessings for a lifetime.

friendship
© 2018 KPT Publishing, LLC
Written by D. A. Michaels

Published by KPT Publishing, Minneapolis, Minnesota 55406
www.KPTPublishing.com
ISBN 978-1-944833-31-2

Designed by AbelerDesign.com

First printing March 2018

10 9 8 7 6 5 4 3 2 1

Printed in the United States of America